A STEP-BY-STEP BOOK ABOUT
PET LIZARDS

RAY STASZKO

Title page: The water dragon (*Physignathus cocincinus*) is not easy to come by but is highly recommended as a pet.

Photographers and artists: William B. Allen Jr., Dr. Herbert R. Axelrod, Horst Bielfeld, Jim Bridges, Richard Crammer, Dr. Guido Dingerkus, Isabelle Francais, Michael Gilroy, Rolf Hackbarth, H. Hansen, Ray Hunziker, Burkhard Kahl, R.J. Koestler, Ken Lucas (Steinhart Aquarium), G. Marcuse, Dr. Sherman Minton, Aaron Norman, Elaine Radford, Mervin F. Roberts.

Humorous drawings by Andrew Prendimano.

Distributed in the UNITED STATES by T.F.H. Publications, Inc., One T.F.H. Plaza, Neptune City, NJ 07753; in CANADA to the Pet Trade by H & L Pet Supplies Inc., 27 Kingston Crescent, Kitchener, Ontario N2B 2T6; Rolf C. Hagen Ltd., 3225 Sartelon Street, Montreal 382 Quebec; in CANADA to the Book Trade by Macmillan of Canada (A Division of Canada Publishing Corporation), 164 Commander Boulevard, Agincourt, Ontario M1S 3C7; in ENGLAND by T.F.H. Publications Limited, Cliveden House/Priors Way/Bray, Maidenhead, Berkshire SL6 2HP, England; in AUSTRALIA AND THE SOUTH PACIFIC by T.F.H. (Australia) Pty. Ltd., Box 149, Brookvale 2100 N.S.W., Australia; in NEW ZEALAND by Ross Haines & Son, Ltd., 18 Monmouth Street, Grey Lynn, Auckland 2, New Zealand; in the PHILIPPINES by Bio-Research, 5 Lippay Street, San Lorenzo Village, Makati Rizal; in SOUTH AFRICA by Multipet Pty. Ltd., 30 Turners Avenue, Durban 4001. Published by T.F.H. Publications, Inc. Manufactured in the United States of America by T.F.H. Publications, Inc.

CONTENTS

Do lizards make good pets? If you are just starting the hobby of keeping lizards as pets, this question is probably foremost on your mind. The prospective seller probably encourages you, but he wants to sell you one. What's the real story?

I got my first lizard 25 years ago. I have had

INTRODUCTION

as many as 20 at one time, including some large and expensive ones kept in a special room set aside for them. For me, they are excellent pets.

On the other hand, many lizards die within weeks or months of purchase. While there is no accurate count, records I have seen would indicate that upward of a million lizards are sold each year worldwide, and probably only a small percentage is alive the following year.

The simple and honest answer to the opening question is that lizards make good to excellent pets *only* if you know a lot about them and are willing to take care of them properly. Fortunately, I can tell you virtually everything you need to know, and will do so in this book. I wish a book of this kind had been available when I started out in the hobby. It could have saved me some money, not to mention some disappointments and several lizard lives.

There are a few books on the market with some good information, but they are incomplete. They spend more time showing you pictures of various lizards and naming them than giving you specific information on their care. This book will of

Opposite: A green spiny lizard (*Sceloporus malachiticus*). Proper management and care of your lizard will help prevent it from becoming another casualty of a well-meaning yet ill-informed owner.

course provide some photos, but it is assumed that you have or will be purchasing your lizard(s) from a pet shop. Consequently, finding out what kind they are will not be a problem. The manager of the pet shop will be able to tell you.

Why should you purchase and read this book? Here are a handful of reasons, facts confirmed by my own experience plus things I have learned from other collectors and competent veterinarians.

1. Most lizards, even ones I would consider worth purchasing, are suffering from one or more of the following: malnutrition, parasites, wounds, bacterial infections. (Stay tuned—all of the foregoing are easily curable.)

2. Most of the traditional foods people feed to lizards (lettuce, hamburger) and even the commonly sold live foods (mealworms, crickets) are not nutritionally complete and may eventually lead to the death of the animals.

3. Most lizards cannot survive indefinitely at the temperatures we find comfortable for our own homes.

4. Few veterinarians are sufficiently knowledgeable about lizards to help you with problems, and the average employee in a pet shop may know even less. Neither is apt to admit this and may lead you astray with guesses.

As a successful lizard owner, you must be part naturalist, part biologist, and part veterinarian yourself. But this is precisely one reason why keeping lizards can be such a rewarding hobby. There is a complexity to the task that requires both knowledge and skill. There is much to learn. You can challenge yourself and acquire a greater appreciation of creatures that are drastically different from us.

HEAT

Probably the least understood and underrated variable in the success of lizard-keeping is temperature. Like many other "cold blooded" creatures, lizards experience changes in the temperature of their surroundings. As their temperature increases, every bodily function is accelerated from digestion to the fighting off of disease organisms. Below a certain temperature, a lizard's body literally does not work. Above a certain

Introduction

Hanging a light bulb outside the terrarium is one way to provide heat; many hobbyists, however, recommend purchasing synthetic "hot rocks" from a pet shop.

temperature, it will go out of control and "crash," somewhat like a race car going too fast around a turn.

So, what's the right temperature? That varies a bit from one type to another and is further complicated by the fact that there is no one correct temperature for any lizard. A lizard must be able to change its temperature by warming up when it needs to and cooling down a bit when it has had enough.

Fortunately, lizards "know" how warm they should be at any point in time. All you have to do is provide a cage that includes a range of temperatures and let the lizard take its pick.

There are various ways to do this. By far the best way, and the only one I recommend, is to purchase from your pet dealer an electrical device designed specially for this purpose. They go under various trade names, but essentially they are synthetic rocks wrapped around small heating coils designed to maintain a controlled temperature that is safe for reptiles. The animals will crawl onto the rock when they need heat and

Rainbow rock skinks (*Mabuya quinquetaeniata*) must not be kept at temperatures below 68°F (20°C).

crawl off it when they have had enough. It's as simple as that. You can leave the devices plugged in constantly all year.

There are other alternatives, but all have disadvantages. Light bulbs produce a scalding heat that will warm the air somewhat but may burn the animals, particularly if they try to crawl onto them. Heating pads designed for humans can be used with care with larger animals, but they often get too hot. You have to be very cautious about electrical safety and possible fire hazards.

Placing cages in the sun is an option, but this must be done with great care. Sunlight is important to lizards; however, by placing a glass or plastic cage in the sun, you risk the same sort of accident that often befalls a dog that is locked in a car in the parking lot of a shopping mall. It is difficult to control or predict how hot it will get inside the cage, and temperatures

may well go into the lethal range. In addition, the whole cage will be heated, so the animals may have no escape. Lizards should not be kept below 70°F (21°C), but once the temperature soars much above 110°F you are flirting with disaster, especially if the heat is inescapable. A lizard should have a means of getting its body heated up into the 90-100°F (32-38°C) range, but not all day long—only when it wants or needs it. Sunlight is neither that reliable nor controllable, especially when it is shining through glass.

I am not suggesting that you avoid letting your lizards get sun. On the contrary, it can be very beneficial, and I will give some tips on how to arrange it. I am saying to *beware* of overheating and not to rely on sunlight as the main source of providing your animal with warmth.

LIGHT

Next to temperature, light probably is the most underrated variable in keeping lizards healthy. There are some noc-

Agamas should be provided with plenty of hiding places in their terrariums. Different species have different requirements as to temperature, light, and humidity.

turnal lizards, such as many geckos, but in general lizards are daytime creatures that spend a lot of time basking in the sun.

One reason they do this is to warm their bodies, but this is not the only reason. Natural sunlight in general and its ultraviolet radiation in particular also are important in keeping the skin healthy and free of infections from bacteria, fungi, or other organisms. Sunlight is also needed by many lizards to maintain skin pigments, especially green lizards such as common iguanas. Perhaps most important, however, sunlight is needed in order to metabolize vitamin D. Most pet lizards suffer from vitamin D deficiency. Its symptoms include deterioration in the quality of skin and bones, curvature of the spine or tail, digestive problems, and reduced resistance to infection. We will talk about the importance of vitamins, and you will learn that you can and should provide vitamin supplements to compensate for, among the other things, the lack of the normal exposure to sunlight.

But you should also provide some carefully controlled exposure to sunlight on occasion and use lighting that comes as close as possible to duplicating sunlight in and around the animals' cages. I have designed special "sun tubes" for some of my lizards. They consist of large sheets of acetate overlay (the transparent plastic used by commercial artists). I roll the sheets and join the edges to form long tubes with diameters of about 8 inches (20 cm). I construct ends for the tubes out of discs of cardboard with large sections cut out and covered with screen to allow good ventilation (very important!). If you use this idea, be sure that your constructions are escape-proof, especially if you plan to use them out-of-doors. I place lizards in the tubes for only about one hour at a time and always make sure that part of the tube is in the shade while the rest is in bright sun, so the lizard can escape from the sun if it begins to overheat. Remember that ultraviolet-B rays do not normally penetrate window glass but will penetrate plastic. (Ultraviolet-A does get through glass but is not as useful to lizards.) However, controlled exposure to sunlight is beneficial even if the ultraviolet component is lacking.

Ultraviolet rays are so important to large lizards such as monitors, however, that I recommend purchasing a tanning

A Nile monitor (*Varanus niloticus*) sunning itself on a rock. Try to let your lizard receive some natural sunlight every day.

lamp with a timer. Take the animals out of glass cages and put them where you can shine the light on them from a distance of 3 feet (1 m) or so (I use the bathtub). I give ultraviolet treatments for about a half hour at a time, two to three times a week. There is a noticeable improvement in skin color and quality, and it tends to make the animals more active and aggressive.

11

NUTRITION & FEEDING

Assuming that you provide your lizard with enough warmth to digest its food and maintain a healthy metabolism, the most important factor in your success or failure as a lizard keeper will be what you choose as a diet for your animal.

Your lizard has lived in the wild for several months—possibly several years—without any help from you or anyone else. It knew exactly how to keep itself alive, including what to eat and how much. Chances are that its ancestors have maintained a particular dietary pattern for millions of years. You cannot maintain that exact pattern, even if you could determine what it was. The specific foods that your lizard ate in the wild simply are not available to you. You must devise a replacement for a million years of successful evolutionary experience. The lizard will eat nothing but what you give it. If the foods you provide are missing a critical ingredient, then sooner or later, in a matter of weeks or months, the deficiency will lead to the downfall of your pet.

When viewed this way, selecting a diet for your pet can be a daunting task. It challenges you and requires that you learn more about reptile nutrition than many people know about human nutrition. Remember that human beings still are "in the wild," meaning that the influence of fellow creatures, plus social tradition and basic instinct, will enable most of us to keep ourselves alive and reasonably healthy, whether or not we know what we are doing.

There is no one diet for all lizards, but there is a lot that can be said that will apply to virtually all of them. Some

Opposite: A green anole (*Anolis carolinensis*) munching on a cricket. A proper diet is essential to the health of your pet lizard.

lizards are predominantly vegetarian or predominantly carnivorous. Others will eat approximately equal amounts of meat and fruits or vegetables, depending upon what they can get. The species summaries will give you some guidance on the preferences of specific lizards.

Let's start with lizards that eat "meat," since most of them do, at least occasionally. You must be particularly careful in selecting a diet for these lizards or you will face tragic consequences. What is "meat" to us can very well be death to a reptile. The meats that we consume—beef, chicken, and the like—generally contain far too much fat to feed to a reptile. Give it hamburger and it will be dead of liver disease within a couple of months. Even cuts we consider lean, such as steak, still contain far too much fat to be given to reptiles on a steady basis unless they are blended carefully with other ingredients.

The best food for any meat-eating animal is a whole animal of the proper size. For larger lizards, this generally means mice; for small lizards, insects. One problem with beef, other than the fat, is that it is made of only one type of body

Gould's monitor (*Varanus gouldi*) devouring a "pinky" or juvenile mouse. Pinkies are safer as a food source than adult mice, since they are too young to fight back.

The black tegu (*Tupinambis teguixin*) can be given pinkies, frogs, and fish; additionally, it is a good idea to offer fruit and raw beaten eggs occasionally.

tissue: muscle. Lizards in the wild are not served steaks or fillets. They must consume whole animals, including skin, bones, blood, and internal organs. Their digestive systems are designed for this purpose.

A lizard that will eat a mouse likely will not require any other food. However, it still will need a vitamin supplement to compensate for lack of sunlight and exercise. I will come to the important topic of vitamins in a moment. Semi-aquatic lizards and crocodilians (water monitors, water dragons, caimans, etc.) also will eat whole live fish such as goldfish.

There are a few comments to be made about feeding mice or other rodents to lizards. Nutritionally, mice may be close to a perfect food, but they do pose problems. First of all, you must consider the size of the rodent relative to the size of the lizard. An active and aggressive monitor or tegu will take on a mouse or rat that is larger than the size of its head and swallow it whole. However, it is not always a good idea for it to do so. Too large a prey may result in damage to your pet. The lizard may later regurgitate the animal. Also, mice and rats will attempt to bite lizards back as they are being grasped, and

15

sometimes they will inflict significant wounds. If a lizard has a bad experience trying to kill a mouse or rat, especially one that was too big to start with, it may become "gun shy" and refuse to go after the next one that is offered.

Some experienced lizard owners and keepers will avoid some of these problems by stunning the prey with a firm blow to the back or neck before offering it to the animal. This is unpleasant at best, since lizards often will ignore dead rodents, so there must still be some signs of life.

A solution I prefer is to try as much as possible to stick with juvenile rodents. Baby mice and rats sometimes are known as pinkies, since they are born without fur. Their eyes are closed, they can barely crawl, and they are altogether quite helpless. Lizards will take them without a fight and generally swallow them whole immediately. Depending upon the sizes of the young rodent and of the lizard, you may wish to offer two or three at a feeding, since lizards that eat mice generally should be fed only every fourth or fifth day. The pattern is for them to fill their stomachs, digest, and excrete, at least partially, before taking another meal.

Sometimes pet shops have and sell "pinkies" as food for lizards or snakes. If not, the best way to guarantee a steady supply is to breed mice yourself. All it takes is putting a male and female together in a cage. They will mate readily and produce anywhere from four to 12 young within a few weeks. By keeping two or three nesting pairs going, you are assured a steady supply at very little cost to yourself. If you plan to keep a large mouse-eater or more than one, it is certainly an option worth considering.

If you cannot obtain rodents or live fish, or if you have a sick animal that cannot or will not eat them, you will have to devise a less "natural" alternative. Many people try to feed lizards a steady diet of dog food, baby food, or some other concoction. This is okay for a couple of weeks if you are trying to revive an emaciated animal. After that, however, the excessive quantity of fat will begin to cause problems.

Strained baby food and canned dog food do offer some advantages in treating a sick animal or a new one that refuses to eat. Sometimes a new animal, even occasionally a healthy

one, may need to be force-fed for a short time until it adjusts to new foods and new surroundings. The best way to do this is to obtain or make a mushy food that is the consistency of strained baby food. You can then use a syringe without a needle (obtainable from any veterinarian) in order to inject the food into the back of the throat where it will be swallowed. All you have to do is get the animal to open its mouth.

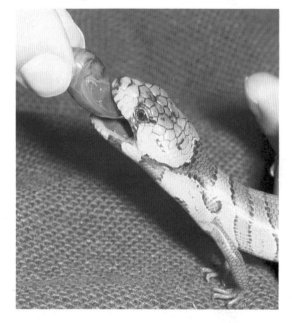

The snail skink (*Tiliqua gerrardi*) will usually prefer snails to any other foods offered. However, its diet should be supplemented with insects and small pieces of meat.

There are various ways of accomplishing this task. An aggressive lizard will open its mouth in defiance if it is picked up or if you gently tap it on the head or neck. However, sometimes it may be necessary to forcibly open the mouth, especially if you are dealing with a sick animal. This operation requires two people: one to open the mouth, the other to inject the food. Sit with the lizard contained (but not crushed) between your knees or thighs. Grasp the nose with the first two fingers of your left hand. Then, with the first two fingers of your right hand, firmly but slowly and carefully pull downward on the skin

below the lower jaw. Some lizards, such as iguanas, have a dewlap (fold of ornamental skin) under their lower jaws. You may take hold of the dewlap right where it attaches to the jaw. With other lizards, such as monitors, you may have to take a scruff of loose skin under the throat. Exert pressure, but be patient. The animal likely will resist at first, but avoid the temptation to pull too hard or you may do damage. Rather, maintain a firm, steady pull without excessive force until the animal weakens and decides to cooperate. In most cases, once the lizard senses food in its mouth it will take it in readily and swallow it.

Another suitable food for large carnivorous lizards is beaten raw eggs. Tegus and some monitors will take to them quite readily, and they may be a good way to "break the ice" and get the animal eating. Being a whole, natural food, they are a better idea than baby food, dog food, and the like. However, try to avoid allowing your animal to adopt an all-egg diet. Try to get it interested in mice, insects, fish, or other protein sources. Incidentally, never try to feed your lizard cooked eggs or meat. Raw foods are always the best.

Girdle-tailed lizards, such as the sun-gazer (*Cordylus giganteus*), should be provided with calcium and vitamin supplements at regular intervals.

A savannah monitor (*Varanus exanthematicus*). Monitors have a tendency to become obese in captivity; therefore, be careful not to overfeed.

Smaller carnivorous lizards generally will eat insects. Unfortunately, insects are not as good a natural food as mice, eggs, or fish, so there are some things you must become aware of if you intend to use insects as a major food source.

The types of insect sold in pet shops—crickets, meal-worms, and superworms—are not necessarily the best types to choose. All of these insects have hard outer shells which make them difficult to digest (small crickets less so than mealworms). The shells can get caught in the intestines of lizards and cause serious problems, especially if the diet is composed entirely of such insects.

Mealworms and superworms (beetle larvae) have an-other annoying and potentially deadly habit. Since lizards generally swallow their food whole with a minimal amount of chewing, these insects are sometimes still alive when they reach the stomach. There they may, and occasionally do, chew a hole in the lining of the stomach while attempting to escape (or maybe they're merely trying to get revenge).

Still, it makes life difficult if you eliminate all of the foods available in pet shops. Occasional feedings of *small* crickets and *small* or freshly molted (very pale in appearance) mealworms will do no harm. The secret of feeding lizards is a varied diet—make your animals eat as many things as possible. The odd cricket will not hurt if your lizard also is getting pinkies, a bit of dog food, some raw eggs, and a fish snack as well.

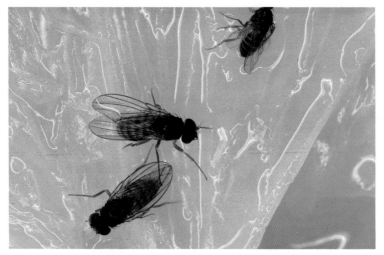

Many hobbyists cultivate their own supply of food animals. Flies, small crickets, and other insects make suitable foods for some lizard species.

Now to the vitamins. All lizards must have vitamin (and probably mineral) supplements. If you do not provide your lizard with vitamins on a steady basis, don't expect it to live longer than a year, regardless of what you feed it. Remember that animals require sunlight (full, unfiltered, including UV) in order to synthesize vitamin D. Lizards also require supplements of calcium and several other vitamins and minerals, including iodine. You can buy powdered vitamin supplements for reptiles in your pet store, but be sure that the one you choose contains

iodine. Otherwise, six months or so down the road your insect-eater may develop goiter.

There are various ways to get powdered vitamin into your pet. If he is aggressive and opens his mouth readily, you may be able to sprinkle it in directly. If so, don't overdo it. Too many vitamins can be as harmful as too little. You want to add very small amounts on a daily basis rather than gulps of the stuff once in a while.

If you plan to feed your lizard live insects or plants that were collected outdoors, be sure they come from an area that has never been sprayed with chemicals.

The best way to proceed is to sprinkle vitamin powder directly onto the food. This works well with moist foods such as fruit, but the powder doesn't stick well to a dry insect. You can try putting a dab of corn syrup on an insect from time to time to get vitamin powders to stick to it. If using mice, try wetting the mouse and then sprinkling it with vitamin supplement just before putting it into the cage. If you want to be clever, you can mix some vitamin powder with honey and smear it onto the mouse's legs or chest. It will then proceed to lick itself clean, thereby swallowing the concoction before it gets swallowed by your lizard.

It is a good idea to try to get insect-eaters to consume some vegetable material. Chances are they do this in the wild, where insects are not always easy to catch and may not always be available. Besides providing vitamins and minerals, the fruits or vegetables seem to help the digestive system.

Sometimes, while a lizard is munching on a superworm or cricket you can slip in a sliver of carrot or a sprig of broccoli. If the lizard shows no interest in eating small pieces of fruit or vegetable on its own, one way to sneak in some is to use certain types of dog food as a supplement. Previously I warned against using dog food as a staple, but it is okay to use it as a supplement with lizards. Pick a brand that is not 100% meat

Close-up of a tokay gecko (*Gekko gecko*). Many lizard species open their mouths as a sign of defense or aggression.

A chuckwalla (*Sauromalus varius*). Chuckwallas are basically vegetarians that will eagerly feed on lettuce, which is suitable as a supplement but not as a staple food, as it is low in nutritional content.

and contains some vegetable material such as corn or cereal. I never give a feeding of all dog food, but I try to work in a few pieces of it along with superworms or other insects, especially for aggressive lizards that open their mouths readily (basilisks, tokay geckos, girdle-tails, and the like).

This brings us to the topic of what to feed vegetarian and partially vegetarian species. The main species that are true vegetarians are green iguanas and chuckwallas, but many other species will eat at least some vegetable material.

The best fruits to offer are banana, melon, grapes, plums, cherries, and other soft, sweet fruits cut into bite-sized pieces. Avoid hard, bitter, or sour fruits or those with an over-abundance of seeds. The best vegetables are spinach, zucchini, squash, shredded carrot, broccoli, and the like. Avoid potatoes, tomatoes, cucumbers and any canned or cooked vegetables. Cabbage may be given occasionally, but many keepers feel it leads to nutritional deficiencies if fed too often.

Nutrition and Feeding

You may have noticed a conspicuous absence of lettuce in the above paragraph. I really would like to say that lettuce should be avoided, because nutritionally it contains less food value than other vegetables. On the other hand, vegetarian reptiles clearly like eating lettuce, perhaps the way children enjoy potato chips. Therefore, it is a useful product when first attempting to induce a new animal to eat. It may also be used mixed in with other fruits and vegetables, but avoid overuse or your animal soon may suffer from malnutrition.

I don't feed any of my vegetarian reptiles on a pure diet of fruits and vegetables. I find that in captivity it is better to offer a more high-powered diet. Particularly for iguanas, I recommend purchasing a bag of dried mynah bird pellets from your pet shop. These are a mixture of vegetables, meat, vitamins, and minerals. Be sure that they also contain fruit, as not all do. Before you can offer these pellets to your lizard, you must soak them in a small amount of water for two hours or so.

My large (44 inches, 130 cm) iguana gets a steady diet of mynah bird pellet mush mixed in with some fresh banana. I feed him every other day, as much as he will eat in a five-minute feeding (which is about when he loses interest). Since my iguana has been trained accordingly, I mix his food in a coffee mug and then feed it to him with a tablespoon. The reason he is responsive to this unusual approach is that when we got him he was quite emaciated from a severe parasite infestation. The way we "rebuilt him" was with daily "forced" feedings of a mush made of mynah pellets, dog food, chopped insects, chopped fresh fruits and vegetables, and a generous vitamin supplement. This regime was so successful that now the lizard is almost unnaturally muscular, very healthy, and active. As a result of the constant handling, he also has become quite tame.

You may find that it is necessary to force-feed your iguana for a few days before it will take the soaked pellets on its own.

Opposite: A leopard gecko (*Eublepharis macularius*) eating a pinky.

A final note: don't leave fruits and vegetables, especially soaked pellets, lying around the cage very long, as they will spoil. Offer fresh food frequently and try to "train" your animal to accept food as soon as it is offered. Daily feedings are recommended for all juvenile and underweight lizards. Larger vegetarians can be fed every second day; rodent-eaters every fourth day, as previously mentioned. Generally speaking, you don't have to worry about lizards overeating and can let them have as much as they want at each feeding (exception: juvenile mouse-eaters). You control obesity by not offering overly frequent feedings, rather than by offering skimpy meals.

WATER

There are only a few things to say about water, but they are so important that your attention should be drawn to them.

Lizards should have a source of *clean* drinking water. It will be clean only if it is changed every day and if the dish or container is washed out often with soap and water. Otherwise, the drinking dish will in reality be a microorganism stew.

A collared lizard (*Crotaphytus collaris*) taking a drink. Be sure to change the water in your lizard's cage every day and to clean the water dish at very frequent intervals.

A green spiny lizard (*Sceloporus malachiticus*). This particular species should not be kept in an environment that is too dry.

Most lizards don't drink an awful lot, so small, shallow dishes are appropriate. Keep only a few dribbles of water on hand at any time, and replenish them when needed. Otherwise, the animals will simply splash water around or tip over the dishes while burrowing, causing the cage to become excessively humid.

There are a few varieties of lizards that sometimes refuse to drink from dishes. They will have to have small amounts of water sprayed or dribbled onto the walls of cages. However, one of the worst habits that many keepers have gotten into is spraying or misting the entire cage. Remember that even lizards like anoles that live in humid climates do not stay soaking wet all day long. If it rains, the hot sun and breezes dry things off quickly. If you spray your lizard's cage, chances are it will stay wet all day, letting bacteria and fungi flourish.

Incidentally, this is one reason why it is often more difficult to keep rain-forest lizards in captivity as compared with desert varieties. It is relatively simple to create a hot, dry environment. However, a humid environment that is also clean and free from infection is more of a challenge. In general lizards that prefer humidity will adapt better to dry conditions than those that prefer dryness will adapt to humidity. You can look after the humidity needs of a lizard such as a common iguana by giving it regular, warm baths. In between, however, it will do better in a *dry* cage.

In designing a cage for your lizard or lizards, there are several things that you must keep in mind. First of all, the design must meet the requirements of the animals. We have talked about heat and light. Humidity is another key variable, and for most lizards this must be minimized. There must be sufficient space for

ENVIRONMENT

the animals to stretch out to their full length and move around. The environment or surroundings must make the animals feel relatively secure in order to minimize the stress of captivity. In other words, a burrowing species should have something to dig in; a climbing variety should have a limb to climb on.

We will discuss the above factors in more detail in a moment, but first we should mention two other factors that often are overlooked. The design must not produce any situation that encourages or permits the animals to harm themselves, and the design must be convenient for you, the owner. Otherwise it will be tedious to keep the cage clean and in good order, and you may fail to do so.

The best way to discuss these considerations is to give some practical examples. In general, you can be very creative in designing or building cages. I have used items as diverse as barrels, dog baskets, and wicker furniture. However, there is a series of *don'ts* that you should use to measure whether or not your proposed plan is, in fact, a good one.

We mentioned humidity. *Don't* allow humidity to build up, or microorganism growth will be rampant and infection the

Opposite: A male green anole (*Anolis carolinensis*). When at ease with its surroundings, the anole's color is green; when disturbed or too cold it turns much darker—brown or almost black.

likely end result. There are several scenarios that can lead to excessive humidity. The most common is to use a glass aquarium tank with a sliding glass top. This type of cage was designed for fish and has some drawbacks for lizards. Spilled water or moisture from food or wastes soon tends to saturate the noncirculating air, especially if a hot rock is in use. If you use a glass aquarium as a cage, be sure to fit it with a screen or mesh top of some sort that will permit air circulation.

Lizards need circulating air, but they should not be placed in drafts. To avoid drafts, it is best to choose a good location for the cage, in a warm spot in the home well away from outside doors and open windows. In such a location you need not, and should not, try to construct an air-tight cage. It is not just a question of fresh air for breathing, but air circulation is necessary to prevent humidity build-up.

I have had good success with constructing wicker cages. They are lightweight and relatively inexpensive. I keep them in a warm room with the door closed. The room is free of drafts, and the natural air circulation keeps the cage quite dry. Added bonuses are that the animals feel more secure in a cage that does not have 100% see-through walls, and they are able to climb the walls, which in effect increases the usable area of such a cage.

Another advantage of wicker, wood, or plastic mesh is that the animals will not harm themselves trying to escape. *Don't* use steel or aluminum screen for the walls of a cage (though for many lizards it is an acceptable material from which to construct a top). The animals will soon have bloodied noses from running the snout back and forth across the screen, trying to get through it.

Another general "don't": *don't* design a cage, however nifty it may seem, that will be difficult to keep clean. I mentioned wicker as good for walls, but it is not suitable as a floor, since food and excrement will get stuck between the fibers. If you use a wicker basket as the base of a cage, cut a cardboard liner for the bottom and change it regularly.

The bottom should always be covered with something removable and disposable. I recommend aquarium sand rather than gravel or aquarium stones. It is easy to remove excrement

Lizard cages should be provided with (depending on the species) branches for climbing, an area for bathing, and, above all, air circulation.

from sand by simply scooping out the surrounding sand with a spoon. This is harder to do with gravel or stones, as waste tends to fall between the rocks and accumulate beneath them.

Don't use dirt or soil. It holds too much moisture and too many bacteria. Also, when it dries it produces such a fine dust that lizards soon become coated with it, and it is a nuisance and a possible hazard for them. Again, clean sand is best. Avoid beach sand, which may be too salty.

The comment about dirt also applies to potted plants. In general they are not a good idea, since the lizards will likely kill them by climbing on them or digging up their roots. For climbing purposes, use sticks or artificial plants. Be sure that they are rigged in such a way that they will support the weight of your animals and provide a solid perch.

Don't tempt your animals to try to escape with loose-fitting tops or large holes or gaps they can poke their heads into. I have seen lizards injure themselves by persistently trying

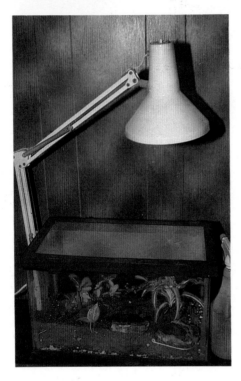

Terrariums for lizards should, in general, not be this crowded; the use of plants is usually discouraged.

to work their heads through small gaps or spaces. The size of any mesh should be calculated so that the animals cannot press their faces into the openings.

Some writers who are, in my opinion, overly concerned about the possibility of mites discourage the use of any wood in cages. It is true that wood is hard to clean and probably should be changed from time to time, but I think it is a good ingredient for a cage, provided it is free of splinters or excessive cracks. Mites are not that difficult to control.

A final consideration: *don't* place anything into a cage that your lizard can crawl into and from which you will be unable to extricate him or which can become a refuge for insects or other live food. Many pet shops sell cholla cactus wood sticks

as decorations and climbing sticks for lizard cages, but they are unsuitable for this purpose. If an anole or curly-tail crawls into the hollow pith, you'll see it again if and when it gets good and ready to come out—not to mention that the wood soon will become a cricket condominium project.

ACTIVITY AND ATTENTION

Many people who admire my reptile collection seem surprised to learn that I do not handle the animals too often, other than to perform routine functions such as cleaning cages or giving baths or sun/UV treatments. I think it comes down to why someone likes reptiles in the first place. If you want an animal to play with or respond to you, you are far better advised to choose a kitten, a puppy, or even a bird or hamster. Reptiles do not play. They do not display affection. Of course, neither do tropical fish, arguably the most popular pets of all time, at least in terms of pet shop sales.

Indeed, for me and (I assume) most reptile keepers, the attraction is that lizards and snakes are wild animals. By keeping them in captivity we take on the challenge of creating an environment for them. Also, we gain a chance to observe and share in the lives of creatures that inhabited this planet many millions of years before the first human being made an appearance. Not only were reptiles around before man, but some common living species of lizards have, in most cases, existed unchanged for millions of years. It is a virtual certainty that long before there were men to name them there were green iguanas, spiny-tailed iguanas, green anoles, savannah monitors, etc. By taking these creatures into our homes we participate in a reality about life on this planet that transcends our own human pursuits and environment. We are reminded of who we are and gain some insight into what this world around us is all about.

This is not to say, however, that it isn't fun to have some influence on the behavior of our pet lizards and other reptiles. Lizards are more intelligent and display a greater ability to learn than many suspect. For example, if a lizard manages to escape from its cage, it will return to the spot where it was successful the first time, obviously remembering how the escape

33

was accomplished. If you feed your animals according to a regular pattern, they will know when you are about to feed them and may come running over to the entrance to the cage, jump toward the top, or make other gestures that indicate both awareness and excitement. Some lizards will look you in the eye and move their heads back and forth to observe your movements.

Accept your pet lizards for what they are. Never become angry or discouraged, for example, if you are bitten. Not all lizards bite, but the ones that do are responding in a proper and logical way. Take it as a sign that the animal is healthy and possesses a will to live. Certainly don't take it personally.

The main advantage of taking lizards out of their cages occasionally is to provide an opportunity for some exercise. This is often the forgotten variable in maintaining the health of your animals. In the wild, lizards must do a certain amount of running around in order to find and catch food and escape from enemies. In captivity they don't need to do either, so they become sluggish and lazy. You'll never catch a lizard jogging.

A green iguana (*Iguana iguana*). Iguanas can inflict painful scratches with their claws, and they often lash out with their tails when frightened.

A collared lizard (*Crotaphytus collaris*) making a run for it. Allow your pet freedom only in a safe, enclosed area, as lizards are notorious escape artists.

They don't get bored or restless. If their bellies are full, they'll likely curl up and take a nap until the next time there seems to be a need to do something. Unfortunately, as for humans, lethargy leads to deterioration of muscles and the possible onset of various health problems.

Placing your lizard in the bathtub or, for example, in a sun tube, wakes it up, gets some adrenaline flowing, and encourages activity. Naturally, you must be sure that your lizard cannot escape, especially small lizards that you may never see again until one day far in the future when you clean out the basement or the back of the closet and come upon the shrivelled remains. I almost never bring my lizards outdoors, due to the risk of their escaping plus the fact that they become exposed to sudden temperature changes and possible environmental hazards (lawn fertilizers, microorganisms, dogs and cats,

and the like). Also, strange situations are stressful to the animals. They become familiar with their cages and sometimes will actually run into their cages when they feel frightened.

Certainly you will want to handle your pet lizards from time to time. However, taking them out with large numbers of people around or passing them back and forth among your friends probably is not a good idea. Respect your reptiles for what they are and adapt your interest to their requirements.

HANDLING PRECAUTIONS

Due to their small size, the lizards that most people keep as pets are not capable of doing any real harm to anyone. About the worst that may happen, with an aggressive species like a basilisk, is that a bite to the finger will puncture the skin and draw a small trace of blood. The way to avoid this is simple: handle aggressive lizards with leather gloves.

If you get into keeping larger and more powerful lizards such as tegus and monitors, however, you will definitely have to take precautions against being bitten. I am told that some large lizards are capable of removing fingers, and I believe it. I have never been wounded by any of my large lizards, simply because I am aware of the danger and never handle them without wearing gloves. However, I occasionally have been careless in handling a baby savannah monitor and have received a couple of painful bites—this despite the fact that the lizard in question was scarcely 8 inches (20 cm) long. Imagine what a three-footer (1 m) could do!

The problem with tegus and monitors is that when they bite you they clamp down and hold on, and their jaws are extremely powerful. If you are ever bitten by one, try hard to avoid the instinct to yank your hand away, as this will lead to tearing and produce a more serious wound. The best way to get the lizard to let go is to submerge its head in water. If you

Opposite: A green iguana (*Iguana iguana*). Some hobbyists prefer to wear gloves when handling their lizards.

A female three-horned chameleon (*Chamaeleo jacksoni*). Never pick up a lizard by the head or by the tail.

are bitten in a pet shop this is easy to do by running to the nearest aquarium. In the home it may be more difficult to find "dunking water" close at hand, unless you have an aquarium. If you have the presence of mind to rush into the bathroom, you can use the tank of the toilet or turn on the tap in the bathtub. The point is that lizards are unable to breathe under water, so will have to let go and come to the surface.

Of course, the advantage of a glove in this situation is that you can usually slip your hand out of the glove, leaving the lizard biting on the hollow leather. I sometimes use a large leather welding glove that has a smaller felt glove inside it, since the felt glove will slide out of the leather fairly easily. The

two combined provide extra protection. Zookeepers use metal-reinforced gloves when handling the real "monsters."

Part of the trick in handling a large lizard safely is knowing how to grab it. Never grab it by the head or the tail, as either move risks injury to the animal. I first go, with my right hand, for the section of back that straddles the front legs. If the animal is prone to thrashing about, I then immediately use the left hand to take hold of the hips. It's a good idea to hold any lizard at arm's length, since it may whip you with its tail or shoot out a little friendly greeting of excrement.

There are some species of lizards that should be handled with gloves not so much because of biting, but because of scratching. Common green iguanas are particularly noted for their sharp claws, and even a relatively small one in a feisty mood can scratch hard enough to draw blood. I don't recommend trying to clip the claws: it is a never-ending chore, and if you clip too deep you cause bleeding and the risk of infection.

A false girdle-tail lizard (*Pseudocordylus microlepitodus*). It is not recommended that the claws of a lizard be clipped, as this practice is more trouble than it is worth.

Lizards are not known for carrying any particularly harmful bacteria. The fact that their skin is dry means they are less at risk to bacterial infections than are turtles or even goldfish. However, all living things have microorganisms on and in them, and bacteria will flourish in any damp environment, especially where excrement or spoiled food is allowed to remain. *All* bacteria are harmful in large quantities. Therefore, use good common sense in handling any wild animals, and wash your hands afterward.

COMPATIBILITY

A short topic but one worth raising. Theoretically, most lizards that are approximately the same size and do not fight with one another can be kept together in the same cage. However, I almost never keep two or more lizards in the same cage, for several good reasons.

First of all, different lizards have different requirements. Some like to climb, others like to dig. I try to design a cage for a specific animal, both its size and its habits. Secondly, lizards are not, by nature, social creatures. They don't get lonely and generally have no use for others of their own species unless it is time to mate—and lizards in captivity rarely do—with some exceptions (anoles, geckos, basilisks). They have no use whatsoever for lizards of another species and will merely see them as unwelcome competitors for food.

The main reason, though, that I generally keep my animals separate is that it enables me to provide a better quality of care and environmental control. Lizards are susceptible to various ailments, many of which are contagious. Beyond that, however, it is also difficult to judge how well an individual is doing in a community cage. For example, it is difficult to tell which animals are eating the food, so it is difficult to ensure that every animal gets its fair share.

If you have more than one lizard of the same species, you may wish to keep them together. If the animals are all healthy, they will be okay so long as you avoid overcrowding, are on the lookout for fighting, particularly between males, and give individual attention to feeding each animal.

Cuban curly-tails (*Leiocephalus carinatus*). Lizards are not gregarious animals, but members of the same species can be kept together if there is plenty of room in the terrarium.

Never let your lizard come into contact with any other type of animal. Dogs and cats are enemies. Turtles often carry amoeba that are harmless to them but deadly to snakes and lizards. Amphibians such as toads and salamanders are often poisonous if eaten.

By now you may have noticed that the standards of care that I recommend in this book are higher than what is practiced by many keepers of lizards, both amateur and professional. But if you aim high when you set your own personal standards, you will find your efforts rewarded with longer lives and a greater percentage of success stories among your reptiles.

One glaring weakness of many publications about reptiles is that they do not pay enough attention to the topic of disease and medicine. While on the one hand I enjoy keeping lizards and recommend them to any serious and responsible pet keeper, I am not one of those who will blandly assure the world that lizards are easy pets to keep alive and healthy. Indeed, this is perhaps a popular misconception. On the whole, I would *not* say that lizards are particularly easy. In fact, I would rank them in the same bracket with tropical fish. They are susceptible to various infections and illnesses, and unless you take an interest in this aspect of their care your chances of long-term success are greatly reduced.

MEDICINE

There are three basic categories of illness that threaten your pet lizards. The first is dietary-related illnesses. They are remedied by following the advice that was presented in the section on nutrition and feeding. If you provide the proper foods, avoid excess fat, use vitamin supplements, and provide warmth and good quality light, you can stay clear of this category with little difficulty.

The next category is infections. There are various contagious conditions that lizards can pass to one another, including bacterial and fungal infections. Fungal infections on or around the skin are evidenced by discoloration of some type. They result from poor sanitation or excessive dampness and often set in as secondary infections in sores or wounds that are not promptly treated. Bacterial infections may show up as swellings around the eyes; sores in and around the mouth; or discharge from the eyes, nose, or mouth. You should note that it is normal for many types of lizards to snort out very small

Opposite: A female sawback agamid (*Calotes calotes*). If you have any doubt about the health of one of your lizards, quarantine it immediately.

quantities of salty liquid from the nostrils. The liquid evaporates, leaving behind salt crystals that may be mistaken for signs of a respiratory disease or "cold." However, a thicker, more mucous discharge that does not promptly evaporate does indicate an infection. Respiratory infections in lizards are serious, but, unlike in humans, they are more commonly bacterial than viral. This means that they can be successfully treated with antibiotics.

The other common type of bacterial infection in lizards involves an overabundance of bacteria in the digestive tract. This commonly occurs when lizards are kept too cold and the food in their stomachs starts to spoil. Since this scenario tends to occur when the animals are warehoused and shipped, you may acquire an animal with this problem. Symptoms include diarrhea and a tendency to regurgitate food for no apparent reason. Rodent-eaters seem particularly prone to this problem. Unfortunately, diarrhea also is a symptom of an even more common digestive ailment: intestinal parasites.

I don't know why the topic of parasites in lizards gets so little attention, since in my opinion it is their number one health menace. Perhaps dealers or pet store owners are afraid that people will be reluctant to buy an animal that may have "worms" in its stomach. Perhaps they are simply ignorant about the magnitude of the problem.

The fact is that a great many lizards are infected with intestinal parasites. Left untreated, many of them will eventually die from the infestation, which gradually saps strength and energy, causing animals to wither away even when they appear to be eating normally. The main symptoms of parasite infestation are lethargy (for example, a normally aggressive species that seems indifferent to being handled); weight loss, especially noticeable at the base of the tail (hips) and hind legs; and poor color and skin quality. Parasite problems are common in green iguanas, and I can now spot an infected animal on first glance by its slender frame, sluggishness, and loss of much of its normal green color to shades of grays and browns. Parasite infestations lead to dehydration, and hence to the lean, dried-out look of the eyes and skin.

Another occasional problem involves mites and ticks.

Ticks are often large, the size and shape of bedbugs. Mites are small and scurry across the scales like tiny moving dots of white or brown. The only time that either poses a serious problem is when a large tick embeds itself close to an eye, where an infection may set in. However, all ticks and mites should be taken seriously and removed or destroyed promptly.

Incidentally, puppies and kittens also suffer from worms, mites, and infections of various types that are similar to those that affect lizards, so you should not jump to the conclusion that lizards are less sanitary than any other pet. On the contrary, parasites in lizards don't tend to infect other animals or humans, whereas some dog and cat parasites can be harmful to humans. Occasionally, but rarely, mites or ticks may carry a virus which can infect humans, causing an illness characterized by fatigue and chronic moderate fever—but don't worry about

A green or emerald lizard (*Lacerta viridis*) that is infested with ticks.

that very much. I have never heard of anyone who has contracted this illness, and even if you do, it is treatable. Still, avoid animals that show signs of ticks or mites, or if you do get one, treat it promptly.

This brings us to the topic of treatment. If you are only buying one small lizard, you may not wish to bother, but if you are or plan to become a serious hobbyist, I recommend that you assemble a lizard first aid kit. Start by buying a bottle of each of the various commercial preparations that are available from good pet stores. For example, there are products used for treating small sores in or around the mouth that also are helpful for bacterial or fungal infection anywhere on the skin. Wormers

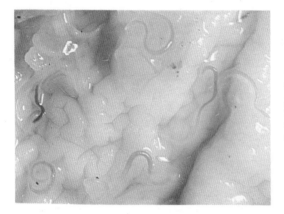

Cross-section of a lizard infested with worms; juveniles and newly imported specimens are particularly at risk from internal parasites.

are given internally to eliminate intestinal parasites. In my opinion, all lizards should be dewormed when they are acquired, whether or not they show obvious symptoms of an infestation. I will explain the procedure in a moment. Other products are used to control mites and ticks.

Round out your kit with a bottle of 3% hydrogen peroxide, some (human) antibiotic first aid creme (such as polysporin), and some clean 3cc syringes—minus the needles (see your veterinarian). I do *not* recommend that you try to give injections to your animals. Leave that to your vet, who is trained to do the job without causing damage, infection, or blood poisioning.

Medicine

External wounds or skin problems, whether bacterial or fungal, can be treated by swabbing the affected area first with hydrogen peroxide, then with an antibiotic creme, following the manufacturer's instructions. The problem is that liquid disinfectants tend to run off or evaporate, so frequent treatments are necessary. For deeper or more persistent sores, a creme such as polysporin is a must.

Ticks and mites can be controlled with commercial products, again following the instructions on the bottle. Usually once you get rid of these pests the first time, they are gone for good. Be careful when removing ticks that you do not rip them apart with your tweezers, leaving the head behind in your lizard, where it may cause an infection. Apply alcohol directly to the ticks, wait a few seconds, then pull on them gently until they let go.

If you have a persistent problem with mites, which is unlikely, or your lizards are kept in cages that contain a lot of wood and are hard to keep totally clean, you can try cutting off a small piece of a cat flea collar or insecticidal vapor strip and suspending it in the cage for two or three days. If you do this, do not allow insects intended as food to stay in the cage before they are eaten. The cage must be adequately ventilated and the lizard should be watched carefully for ill effects.

Internal bacterial infections of either the digestive or respiratory system require the assistance of a veterinarian. Search long and hard and find one who has proven experience with reptiles. Not all products used on dogs and cats are safe for lizards. The best antibiotics are chlorpalm and bactrim. They come as a chalky liquid that you must gently force into your lizard's mouth through a syringe. Simply dabbing it on food is not satisfactory. Pet shops sell tetracycline capsules intended for treating aquariums, but I do not recommend using them on lizards as it is difficult to calculate a proper dosage. Gentocin is an effective antibiotic administered by injection only.

The best medicines for intestinal parasites are thiabendazole or fenbendazole (sold under various trade names), which are available from many pet shops and any veterinarian. Avoid using any other dog or cat wormers, as they may kill your lizard! Also, you and your vet should be aware that the dosage is

different for lizards than for dogs, since lizards have a slower digestive cycle. Lizards get a one shot dosage (50mg per kilo body weight) that may be repeated two weeks later when any eggs left behind should have hatched.

The proper treatment for protozoan infections is metronidazole, at a one-time dosage of 250 mg per kilogram. Metronidazole has also proved to be an effective appetite stimulant for snakes and for lizards such as monitors and tegus, whether or not an illness is present. As a stimulant, the dosage is halved to 125 mg/kilo.

A final category of problems involves infection and possibly even gangrene in extremities, mainly fingers, toes, or the tip of the tail. This is a problem where animals kept together fight, where sanitation is poor, or where animals experience poor circulation due to excessively low temperatures. Sometimes the animals bring the problem on themselves by biting their own fingers, perhaps to help remove shed skin.

If an appendage dies, it must be amputated or the situation will spread to the surrounding tissue. This is a matter best left for a vet. If you do decide to amputate a swollen finger, be aware that it will bleed profusely unless you first apply a tourniquet. Tie a piece of sturdy, clean string or thread tightly around the digit just inside of where you plan to cut. Be sure that your cut is in far enough to remove all of the dead or infected tissue, but go no farther than necessary. Cut the digit with sharp scissors that have first been sterilized in boiling water. Coat the exposed tip with an antibiotic creme such as polysporin. To keep the wound clean for the first couple of days and to prevent the animal from damaging the scab, I recommend that you make a makeshift "cast" using a piece of sticky nylon-reinforced tape. Run it along the bottom of the hand or foot, then bend it up around the end and over the top. Apply only gentle pressure in securing the tape to the lizard's skin, but then stick the outer edges of the bottom layer to the outer edges of the top layer, which is the main thing that will keep the "cast" on. After about three days you can remove both the cast and the tourniquet by soaking the animal in warm water for several minutes, then gently pulling and/or cutting the bandage. Apply antibiotic (polysporin) to the exposed tip for about a week thereafter.

Many lizards can lead contented lives after a toe or a limb has been amputated. This particular animal can still move and hunt for its prey without difficulty.

I have personally performed this procedure several times and have never had a failure yet. Once a finger becomes battered and swollen, it is often the only way of removing the infection and saving the rest of the hand.

I am not sure if the lizard feels pain during the amputation, but anesthetics for reptiles are a complex subject. Many anesthetics may be more harmful—even deadly—than either the gangrene or amputation. If you are squeamish or local humane laws prevent such home surgery, let your vet do it.

Once you've successfully treated your animal, sanitation is the key to preventing recurrences. You must keep the cage clean. If the animals become stained with dried excrement, give them a warm bath and if necessary scrub them off with an old toothbrush. Also, keep cages dry, since bacteria, fungi, and most parasites require a moist environment to survive. Incidentally, warm baths are also helpful when an animal has difficulty shedding skin, as are ultraviolet treatments.

People who collect lizards learn that they are as different in their nature and "personalities" as people. In this final section, I will give you my personal "reviews" on the lizards I have encountered or about which I have received first-hand reports. There will be no hearsay here, so if you don't see a specific type of lizard in the following listing, it is merely because I personally have never come across one and so do not feel entitled to an opinion. It is hoped that the following comments will help you select a type of lizard that will match your expectations and interests. Please remember that every type of lizard has its fans, and perhaps my experiences have not all been typical. Solomons skinks and chuckwallas, for example, are prized pets of many keepers who have had excellent luck with them.

PICKS AND PANS

Agamas These include various species of *Agama* and allies. I have had a red-headed agama *(Agama)* and a horned mountain agama *(Acanthosaura)* and have been disappointed with both. They definitely require high heat and don't seem to take well to captivity or the types of foods commonly available. The red-headed agama is also particularly fast moving, prone to bolting from the cage when you lift the lid, and may attempt to bite when grabbed. Red-headed agamas frequently have a black discoloration on the tail that apparently is harmless, as I have seen it on many otherwise healthy specimens. They eat insects and may take some vegetation.

Anoles These small lizards (*Anolis carolinensis,* etc.) are most appropriate for uninterested parents looking for an inexpensive lizard with a short life span so they can discourage the

Opposite: A pair of green anoles (*Anolis carolinensis*). Green anoles are among the most common of all lizards seen in captivity.

hobby. You probably could pave the nation with the dead little anoles (also called American chameleons) of the last three generations of young pet keepers. Serious collectors seldom bother with them. If you can get a freshly caught healthy one, there is no good reason why you shouldn't be able to keep it alive for a couple of years if you provide warmth and a diet of a variety of small insects (not just mealworms) and spiders. If the lizard won't go for a cricket readily, there is something wrong with it—don't buy it. They tend to be avid eaters.

Basilisks The brown or common basilisk *(Basiliscus basiliscus)* is one of the more commonly available species, and any large collection would be incomplete without one. However, if it is the first lizard you buy, you may very well be disappointed and never get another one. They can be quite ill-tempered, especially the males, and their bite will draw blood. They

A double-crested basilisk (*Basiliscus plumifrons*). This species is the most delicate of the basilisks.

A chameleon is considered by many to be too delicate for a beginning hobbyist. Above all, it must not be overhandled.

generally eat readily, even snatching crickets from your hand, especially if they have a hot rock to warm themselves. If one won't eat readily, there's something wrong, so don't buy it. This is one of very few lizards that is easy to breed in captivity. In fact, large females often have eggs when purchased, though younger females may lay eggs that are infertile. If you end up with eggs, keep them warm (100°F, 38°C) in moist sand or peat moss for several weeks until they show signs of developing or rotting. Basilisks eat insects readily. Try to force in some vegetation and vitamins now and then.

Chameleons I mean here the Old World types with bug eyes and prehensile tails *(Chamaeleo)*. No, no, no, leave the poor things alone. They have enough problems. If people would stop buying them, people would stop catching them (with tongs, of all things, leaving nasty wounds on their backs) and there would be a lot fewer dead lizards going out with the trash. Probably the hardest of all lizard species to keep alive in captivity. If you're a die-hard addict determined to beat the odds, you'll have to provide a large cage with plenty of branches to climb on and high dry heat (forget hot rocks—they won't stay on them). You'll have to heat the air in the cage to 95°F (35°C). Provide numerous small flying insects such as fruit flies or mosquitoes at all times, along with moths, crickets, and larger insects, and avoid the urge to overhandle, as this is stressful to such a delicate creature.

A conehead (*Laemanctus longipes*). Coneheads are known for their drastic color changes.

Chuckwalla A neat lizard *(Sauromalus obesus),* but hard to keep alive for long. At least, I've had bad luck with them and probably won't try again. The trouble is that in the wild they are heat-loving vegetarians, and they are partial to certain specific plants in their natural habitat. They are often slow to accept substitutions. Young ones in captivity will eat crickets, but I'm not sure they ought to. If anyone has one that he has kept alive for longer than two years, I'd like to hear about it.

Collared Lizard *Crotaphytus collaris* is a really good basic, hearty lizard, easy to feed and keep alive, interesting to watch, and reasonably calm when handled. Triple A rating. They eat insects.

Coneheads *(Laemanctus)* Definitely the winner in the not-very-bright category. May require force-feeding. Love to climb and jump on people's heads. Docile, medium-sized, reasonably priced. Probably won't live long. I tend to stay away from those skinny-legged varieties, which also include the helmeted lizards *(Corytophanes).*

Picks and Pans

Crevice Spiny Swift *(Sceloporus poinsetti)* A better lizard than the other swifts for about the same price. Colorful and easy to keep. May not eat well at first, but should come around soon and eat readily. Recommended. Eats insects.

Curly-tails *(Leiocephalus)* Next to *Anolis,* the most commonly available species in pet shops. These are a better deal than anoles because they are easy to keep alive. However, they are fast runners and their tails come off easily, so be careful trying to handle them. Males also are surprisingly aggressive. Eat insects. An okay starter lizard, except that children may be disappointed that they are so hard to handle.

Caimans Strictly speaking not lizards, these crocodilians *(Caiman crocodilus)* belong on this list anyway. For serious collectors only. Aggressive, fast-growing, and difficult at the best of times, but a true thoroughbred. Needs heated, filtered water, ample space, and dry rocks to crawl out onto, preferably under a full-spectrum lamp. Beware of bacteria or fungi building up on the skin, especially on the tail. I learned this the hard way when one of mine had to have part of its tail amputated. Now I keep it in a dry pail every second night to be sure that it dries out thoroughly. Eats live fish (goldfish)— lots of live fish—and needs mice pinkies and vitamins.

The caiman *(Caiman crocodilus)* is actually a member of the alligator family. Caimans are very aggressive, even at a young age.

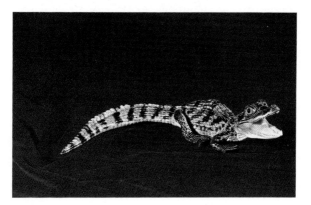

A male sawback agamid (*Calotes calotes*). This species is known for its bright coloration and extremely long tail.

Calotes *(Calotes)* A strange beast capable of changing colors dramatically if it gets angry or upset. Mine gets angry rather easily, bobbing its head up and down, extending its large dewlap (throat flap), turning literally blue in the face, and sometimes even striking the glass. If you're into this sort of thing, go for it. Eats insects.

Cuban Anole *(Anolis equestris)* One "ugly dude" with a powerful bite and a nasty temper. They seem to be constantly shedding skin. Not my cup of tea, but to each his own. Eats insects. Likes to climb.

Fat-tailed Gecko *(Hemitheconyx)* If you're into geckos (I'm not), this is the Rolls Royce, along with the leopard *(Euble-*

pharis) gecko. Expensive, nocturnal, insect-eating, fairly easy to keep alive, but at that price, you'll weep when it dies. The leopard gecko, on the other hand, currently is cheap because it is being captive-bred and has much the same attributes.

Girdle-tail Lizard *(Cordylus)* Fast-moving and nasty-tempered (the only one of my lizards that's bitten me more often is the tokay gecko), but they are fine looking beasts and fairly easy to keep. I "force-feed" mine a combination of live insects and dog food and he is thriving. In this case force-feeding is easy, because every time I catch him, he opens his mouth in protest. When I drop food in, he takes it and swallows it readily. This feeding technique works fairly well on any aggressive lizard, but once you start it, you may have to keep doing it, because it may not be interested in eating on its own.

Green Iguana *(Iguana iguana)* The most identifiable of all lizards, and perhaps the perfect reptile pet, but only if you are willing to devote a lot of time to it. My favorite lizard at present is a 42-incher (107 cm). When I got him he was skin and

A fat-tailed gecko (*Hemitheconyx caudicinctus*). This species is expensive compared to the more commonly available leopard gecko.

bones, suffering from a severe infestation of parasites plus bacterial infections around the eyes and the tips of two fingers (which ultimately required amputation). He was successfully rebuilt by treatments with wormer and antibiotic; daily "force-feedings" with a mush composed of moistened mynah bird pellets, dog food, and crushed fresh fruits and vegetables with vitamins and powdered protein added for good measure; plus daily baths and half-hour sessions under a sun lamp. Unless you're prepared for this kind of challenge, be sure you get a healthy one (they aren't cheap). When first acquired, your iguana should run from you as you try to pick it up, raise itself up, and whip you with its tail. If it's passive from the start, there's something wrong. You have to tame it by constantly handling it until it gets used to you. From my experience, not all iguanas can be tamed. A healthy specimen will do fine on a strictly vegetarian diet with vitamin supplements and a source of full-spectrum light. They like to swim and should be given warm (90°F, 32°C) baths daily. Watch for signs of parasites, as they are particularly susceptible to them. By the way, large iguanas can give nasty scratches (without really meaning to) with their powerful claws. I'm told that they sometimes bite, but I have never been bitten by one. As lizards go, they are very intelligent and about as responsive as any pet reptile ever gets (but don't expect it to fetch a ball.)

Monitors *(Varanus)* If you collect lizards, sooner or later you'll give in and get a monitor. You'll hear about water monitors that reach a length of over 10 feet (3 m). Now *that's* a lizard! But you may be disappointed. Monitors can be nasty-tempered and get large enough to do serious damage with their powerful jaws. They are susceptible to bacterial eye and respiratory infections, which should be treated promptly. I also got one monitor that turned out to be loaded with intestinal parasites. Small monitors eat mice (one or two a week), large ones chickens and rabbits. They require warmth. Water monitors and Nile monitors should be given warm baths like iguanas. Savannah monitors and the like should be kept dry. They need a source of ultraviolet light. Placed in the sun, they become aggressive and prone to snapping (which is, after all,

A sailfin lizard (*Hydrosaurus amboinensis*). This species is known for its huge appetite—if it doesn't eat willingly, don't buy it!

their true nature). You can get them to tolerate handling, but they never become particularly responsive. They need heat to digest food, and without it food may spoil in their stomachs (a problem that can affect other types of lizards as well). They are avid eaters, and I do recommend them for serious and responsible collectors. Savannah monitors are my favorite.

Sailfin Lizard *(Hydrosaurus)* These look fragile, but they are interesting and responsive medium-sized lizards that I recommend. They should pounce at food, even in the pet shop, or

A black or spiny-tail iguana (*Ctenosaura pectinata*). Spiny-tails should not be too passive, as they are somewhat aggressive by nature.

don't buy. They eat like pigs, just about anything—insects, vegetables, and they are particularly fond of fresh fruits such as plums, grapes, and melon. They need the same type of cage as is described for the water dragon, though it need not be as large.

Skinks Fairly easy to handle and keep alive. Some are tamer than others. Most eat readily (primarily insects). Some can be fast moving, and all are escape artists. Many are livebearers, so if you buy a chubby female there is a chance that a baby lizard will appear in the cage one day. If so, feed it ants and tiny insects. These are not the most exciting lizards in the world, but they are recommended due to their ease of care. They seem to tolerate room temperature conditions better than most species.

Solomons Skink (*Corucia zebrata*) I have only come across three of these, and none of them lasted very long. They are interesting animals with powerful limbs, a prehensile tail, and sharp claws. Gloves are a must. They like to climb. These lizards are omnivorous, but away from their natural diet they seem to become constipated easily, and they suffer other types of gastrointestinal problems. Not recommended.

Picks and Pans

Spiny-tailed Agamid (*Uromastyx*) This lizard is difficult but worth the effort. It is tame and friendly unless it is startled, when it can cause a nasty wound with a quick flip of its armored tail. Mainly a vegetarian, it should also be given some animal protein, such as top quality dog food. It may require hand-feeding. This lizard requires exceptionally high heat, in the 90–100°F range. This can best be provided with a 40 or 60 watt light bulb, which should be surrounded with mesh to prevent the lizard from scalding itself against the bulb, along with a "hot rock." A sandy bottom is preferred, deep enough for the lizard to burrow into. This lizard is very susceptible to respiratory infections, especially if the cage is damp or too cool. However, like several other species, it secretes salt crystals at the nostrils, which are not to be confused with respiratory fluid.

Spiny-tail Iguana *(Ctenosaura)* Not quite as nice as a green iguana, but highly recommended nonetheless. They vary in size and temperament. Some are totally passive, others prone to biting; once again, being too passive is not a good sign. Eats insects and may eat some vegetation; may accept dog food as a supplement to live food; large ones may take mice.

Sudan Plated Lizard *(Gerrhosaurus major)* Not easy to find, but a great lizard. Larger than the yellow plated *(G. flavigularis)* and more interesting. Eats well (insects and fruit), fairly tame, and handleable. Mine had intestinal parasites and a bacterial build-up on the skin when I got it, but both problems were easily cured.

Swifts *(Sceloporus)* There are dozens of varieties of swifts that are readily available and inexpensive, and I don't have any (except the crevice spiny). Perhaps that says something. I find them ordinary, and I happen to have had bad luck with two multicolored swifts that died for no apparent reason. They're all small, and many are fast moving. Some are also surprisingly aggressive for their size. Don't buy one if it won't go for a cricket readily or if any of the others in the cage seem abnormal or emaciated.

Tegu *(Tupinambis)* Large and real nasty, a genuinely dangerous lizard, but I have two of them. Eat mice, rats, and stray fingers. In some ways they seem heartier than monitors. They

A collared lizard (*Crotaphytus collaris*).

love raw eggs but get hooked on them and may refuse to eat rodents thereafter. The Chilean dwarf tegu *(Callopistes)* is a good smaller lizard that is aggressive without being dangerous.

Tokay gecko *(Gekko gecko)* One "mean dude," but no collection is complete without one. Bites so hard it is painful through leather gloves, even though specimens longer than a foot are uncommon. Like most geckos it is nocturnal, so provide a cage with dark hiding spots. Seems to tolerate room temperature. I force insects and dog food, but they will generally eat well on their own, either insects or baby "pinky" mice. Like most geckos they can run up the wall and across the ceiling, so handle with care. Definitely *not* for children.

Water dragon *(Physignatus cocincinus)* Hard to come by, but jump at the chance if you get it. A really fine lizard and easy to care for (despite rumors to the contrary). Needs a large cage and a pan of water it can bathe in (keep it clean), as well as a hot rock or other heat source. They love superworms, and I coax mine by hand to eat small goldfish and some vegetable material doused in vitamin powder. Watch for fungus infections. Be aware that this lizard has sharp teeth and powerful jaws, though mine has never bitten me. They have a striking look to them, green with orange and hints of other colors, with a row of soft spikes down the back and white lumps around the jaw. Moderately large and often reasonably priced. Triple A rating.

SUGGESTED READING

THE COMPLETELY ILLUSTRATED ATLAS OF REPTILES AND AMPHIBIANS FOR THE TERRARIUM
By Fritz Jurgen Obst, Dr. Klaus Richter, and Dr. Udo Jacob
ISBN 0-86622-958-2
TFH H-1102

Here is a truly comprehensive and beautiful volume covering all reptiles and amphibians any hobbyist (or scientist) is likely to ever see or want to know about. The alphabetical arrangement makes it easy to find information on almost any topic, and the more than 1500 full-color photos make this book a pleasure to look at as well.

ENCYCLOPEDIA OF REPTILES AND AMPHIBIANS
By John F. Breen
ISBN 0-87666-220-3
TFH H-935

This book provides enormous coverage of the care, collection, and identification of reptiles and amphibians. Broken down by animal type, it is written for either the amateur or professional herpetologist, making it of value to anyone interested in herptiles. Contains 316 black and white and 267 color photographs.

BREEDING TERRARIUM ANIMALS
By Elke Zimmermann
ISBN 0-86622-182-4
TFH H-1078

This volume covers everything the hobbyist needs to know about the successful breeding and rearing of terrarium animals, including housing, terrarium, light and heat, breeding food animals, and many other essential topics. In addition to the superlatively informative text, this book contains over 200 full-color and black and white photos.

INDEX